He's Your Daddy!

Ducklings, Joeys, Kits, and More

By Charline Profiri
Illustrated by Andrea Gabriel

Dawn Publications

For young ones and their daddies.—CP

For Janna, without whom many grand adventures would have been less grand.—AG

Library of Congress Cataloging-in-Publication Data

Names: Profiri, Charline, author. | Gabriel, Andrea, illustrator.
Title: He's your daddy : ducklings, joeys, kits, and more / by Charline
Profiri ; illustrated by Andrea Gabriel.
Other titles: He is your daddy
Description: First edition. | Nevada City, CA : Dawn Publications, [2018] |
Audience: Ages 3-8. | Audience: K to grade 3.
Identifiers: LCCN 2017043286 | ISBN 9781584696254 (hardback) | ISBN
9781584696261 (pbk.)
Subjects: LCSH: Animals--Infancy--Juvenile literature. |
Animals--Nomenclature--Juvenile literature. |
Animals--Identification--Juvenile literature.
Classification: LCC QL762 .P76 2018 | DDC 591.3/92--dc23 LC record available at https://lccn.loc.gov/2017043286

Book design, ebook, and computer production by
Patty Arnold, *Menagerie Design & Publishing*

Manufactured by Regent Publishing Services, Hong Kong
Printed July, 2018, in ShenZhen, Guangdong, China

10 9 8 7 6 5 4 3 2 1
First Edition

Dawn Publications
12402 Bitney Springs Road
Nevada City, CA 95959
www.dawnpub.com

Baby animals, wild or tame,
Don't always have their daddy's name.

If you were a *pup* exploring a log,
Your daddy might be a furry, brown *dog*.

If you were a *joey*, a piggyback rider,
Your daddy might be a sweet *sugar glider*.

If you were a *cygnet* waking at dawn,
Your daddy would be a graceful, white *swan*.

If you were a **fry**, so teeny tiny,
Your daddy might be a **seahorse** that's spiny.

If you were a *kit* with teeth like a cleaver,
Your daddy might be a wood-chomping *beaver*.

If you were a *hatchling* peeping in a nest,
Your daddy might be a *robin redbreast*,

OR . . .

a DINOSAUR!

If you were a **duckling** afloat on a lake,
Your daddy would be a colorful **drake**.

If you were a sweet, adorable *calf*,
Your daddy might be a towering *giraffe*.

If you were a **tadpole** swishing in a bog,
Your daddy might be a speckled, green *frog*.

If you were a spotted, skinny-legged *fawn*,
Your daddy might be a *stag* on the lawn.

If you were a *kitten* sprawled on a mat.
Your daddy might be a curious *cat*.

But you are a *child* with a *daddy*, too.
Whatever you call him, he's special to you.

He's your daddy!

EXPLORE MORE—For Kids

Matching Game

Directions: Use your finger to draw a line from the baby animal to its daddy.

1. Pup   A. Giraffe

2. Joey   B. Swan

3. Cygnet   C. Robin

4. Fry   D. Stag

5. Kit   E. Seahorse

6. Hatchling   F. Cat

7. Hatchling   G. Frog

8. Duckling   H. Dog

9. Calf   I. Drake

10. Tadpole   J. Sugar glider

11. Fawn K. Dinosaur

12. Kitten L. Beaver

Answers: 1-H, 2-J, 3-B, 4-E, 5-L, 6-C, 7-K, 8-I, 9-A, 10-G, 11-D, 12-F

More About the Animals

Running, jumping, and climbing help a **pup** grow strong. There are 340 different types (breeds) of dogs in the world. The **dog** in this book is a golden-doodle.

Sugar gliders are small marsupials that live in Australia. They glide through the trees at night. Sweet sap is one of their favorite foods. A **joey** starts to ride piggyback two weeks after leaving its mother's pouch.

A **cygnet** (*sig-net*) can walk as soon as it hatches. It begins to swim its first day. A cygnet has light gray or brown feathers until it is two years old. Most adult **swans** are all white.

A **seahorse** is a fish that lives in the ocean. A female seahorse lays eggs in a male seahorse's pouch. After two weeks, the eggs hatch and tiny **fry** leave their daddy's pouch.

A **beaver kit** begins to swim soon after it's born. Beavers can see underwater because their eyelids are transparent. Beaver teeth never stop growing. But because they gnaw on trees, their teeth are kept from getting too long.

An American **robin** is sometimes called a "robin redbreast." Robin **hatchlings** weigh less than a quarter. Both parents work together to feed them 100 meals a day.

The **dinosaur hatchling** shown in this book is a Triceratops. It hatched from an egg the size of a cantaloupe. Triceratops lived about 65 million years ago. They were the largest of the horned dinosaurs.

A **duckling** is a baby duck. Daddy ducks are called **drakes**. The bright green head and yellow bill of the drake in this book show that it's a mallard duck.

A **giraffe** is the tallest animal in the world—up to 20 feet tall (6 meters). A newborn **calf** is 6 feet tall (2 meters). Every giraffe has a different fur pattern—no two giraffes are the same.

Tadpoles hatch from eggs laid in water, and they live completely underwater for a few weeks. Their bodies go through a change (metamorphosis). Then they become **frogs** and are able to breathe air.

A **fawn** is a baby deer. Its spotted coat helps it stay hidden from predators. A **stag** is a daddy deer. Stags begin to grow antlers in the spring and shed them in the winter.

Cats have lived with people for thousands of years. They are natural hunters like lions and tigers, their much bigger cousins. Cats sleep more than most mammals. **Kittens** may sleep 20 hours a day.

Parental Care—What Does Daddy Do?

All animals have two parents, but animal dads usually don't play a major role in raising their families. Mothers typically do most of the work of taking care of babies and getting them ready to survive on their own. This is true of many of the animals in this book. Male giraffes, frogs, deer (stags), and ducks (drakes) do not interact with their babies. And although male dogs and cats sometimes play with their young, they do not take care of them. Seahorse dads play a unique role in giving birth to their young, but the fry are completely on their own as soon as they leave the pouch.

However, some daddies do help out. Sugar glider males help take care of joeys after they leave the mother's pouch. Robin dads work together with the moms to feed and protect the babies while they're in the nest. And male swans will protect their cygnets for about six months. Beaver kits live in extended families with both parents and older siblings for two years before leaving to find a mate.

At home or in the classroom, this book may spark conversations about human dads. As the traditional nuclear family has changed over the years, the role of "daddy" is sometimes fulfilled by others, including grandfathers, uncles, or older brothers.

Or Daddy Could Be . . .

What kind of animal is a daddy for a pup? In this book, the daddy is a dog. But more than 20 other animals have babies that are called pups. How many do the children know? Bring in photos of the unusual animals, such as the agouti.

Some animals who have the same baby name may look alike (dog and wolf), while others look very different (dog and dolphin). Have children compare some of the animals by creating Venn diagrams.

BABY	DADDY	OR DADDY COULD BE...
Pup	Dog	Agouti (uh-GOO-tee), anteater, armadillo, bat, bearcat, coyote, dolphin, fox, gerbil, guinea pig, hamster, hedgehog, mole, mouse, otter, prairie dog, rat, seal, shark, squirrel, walrus, wolf
Joey	Sugar Glider	Kangaroo, koala, Tasmanian devil, wallaby, wombat
Cygnet	Swan	No other animal has a baby called a cygnet.
Fry	Seahorse	All other types of fish
Kit	Beaver	Badger, ferret, fox, honey badger, mink, muskrat, rabbit, skunk, squirrel, weasel, woodchuck
Hatchling	Robin and Dinosaur	Alligator, crocodile, emu, snake, turtle, and all other types of birds
Duckling	Drake (male duck)	No other animal has a baby called a duckling.
Calf	Giraffe	Aardvark, addax, antelope, beluga, bison, bongo, buffalo, camel, caribou, cow, dolphin, elephant, elk, gnu, hippopotamus, manatee, moose, ox, porpoise, reindeer, rhinoceros, whale, yak
Tadpole	Frog	Toad
Fawn	Stag	Pronghorn
Kitten	Cat	Beaver, bearcat, bobcat, rabbit, raccoon, rat, squirrel

Tips For Reading Aloud

1. Preview the book *He's Your Daddy* ahead of time. Engage the child by reading with expression. Use a soft or loud voice and emphasize the rhyme.

2. Read the title and identify the author and illustrator. Explain what each one does. Examine the cover illustration. *Which animal is the daddy? Which one is the baby? The baby animal is called a joey. The daddy is called a sugar glider. Ducklings and kits are names of other animal babies.* Ask children to make predictions of what the book is about.

3. Read aloud the entire text *He's Your Daddy* with few interruptions. Pause to provide the meanings of unfamiliar words.

4. Have children review their predictions. *What is the book about? What information does the author give you?*

5. Read the book again. For each animal rhyme, ask children to use the illustrations and the text to identify each baby animal and its name, and the daddy and its name. Have children identify the rhyming words.

6. Discuss the differences between wild and tame animals. Look back at the illustrations of each animal. *Which animals are tame? Which animals are wild? How did you decide whether an animal is tame or wild? The dinosaur, a Triceratops, was once wild but is now extinct.*

Science

Parents and Offspring—Babies are like their parents in some ways, but different in other ways. After reading the book, return to the illustration of the swan. Ask children how the babies are the same or different from their daddy. *(Same—both have feathers, both have a beak, both have two feet, both have two wings. Different—the daddy is bigger than the babies, the daddy has longer feathers on his wings, the daddy has a black beak and legs but the babies have a pink beak and legs.)* Compare babies and daddies in other illustrations. Notice some babies are very similar to their dads *(pup/dog)* and others are very different *(tadpole/frog)*. For older children, you may expand the lesson by exploring animal life cycles, such as: hatchling—fledgling—robin; fawn—yearling—deer; eggmass—tadpoles—froglet—adult frog. Supplement the stages that are not shown in the illustration with additional pictures. (NGSS 1-LS3-1: Heredity: Inheritance and Variation of Traits).

Math

Adding and Subtracting Babies—Have children practice adding or subtracting by using the number of babies for two different species. To determine which species will be used in the math problem, have a child randomly draw two bookmarks out of a box. (Bookmarks are available as a free download at www.dawnpub.com/activities.) Using the list below, create an age-appropriate math problem based on the number of babies for each animal. For example: 6 pups + 6 kits = 12 babies, or 8 cygnets – 3 hatchlings = 5 babies.

Dog—5-6 puppies, up to 8

Giraffe—1 calf

Swan—3-8 cygnets, up to 12

Seahorse—as few as 5 fry, up to 2,500

Beaver—1-6 kits

Robin—3-4 hatchlings

Dinosaur—unknown

Duck—1-13 ducklings

Sugar Glider—1-2 joeys, up to 4

Frog—thousands of tadpoles

Deer—1-2 fawns, occasionally 3

Cat—3-5 kittens, up to 10

Educators: There are many useful resources online for most of Dawn's books, including activities, bookmarks, and standards-based lesson plans. Scan this code to go directly to activities for this book, or go to www.dawnpub.com and click on "Activities" for this and other books.

Charline Profiri is a former K-3 teacher who began writing for children after her early retirement. Her books make learning fun! The idea for *He's Your Daddy* came when Charline read a list of baby animals with different names than their parents. Charline has lived in California, New Mexico, New York, Wisconsin, and Saudi Arabia. She currently lives in Arizona. She loves travel and has visited 19 countries. Her other favorite activities are learning, reading, swing dancing, aqua aerobics, and reconnecting with children via school and library presentations. She is the award-winning author of *Counting Little Geckos* and *Guess Who's in the Desert*. Visit Charline's website to book an author visit, download teaching guides, or for more information. www.cprofiri.com

Andrea Gabriel has been illustrating children's nature books for nearly 20 years. She grew up surrounded by scientific and artistic adults who gave her both a passion for the outdoors and the desire to portray her experience in drawings and paintings. The illustrations for this book were created with both watercolor and digital techniques. Andrea hopes that her work will help young people develop the same love for the natural world and its inhabitants that her parents gave to her. She lives in Bellingham, Washington, with her family of two- and four-footed creatures. This is Andrea's second book for Dawn. She also illustrated *Daytime Nighttime, All Through the Year*. See more of her art at andreagabriel.com.

More Nature Awareness Books from Dawn Publications

Daytime Nighttime, All Through the Year—Delightful rhymes depict two animals for every month, one active during the day and one busy at night. See all the action!

Baby on Board: How Animals Carry Their Young—Tucked in pouches, gripped in teeth, propped on backs, or underneath—these are just some of the clever ways animals carry their babies.

Over in the Ocean: In a Coral Reef—A coral reef is a marine nursery, filled with mamas and babies. Children will count and clap to the rhythm of "Over in the Meadow" while reef animals flutter, puff, and dart.

Tall Tall Tree—There's a world teeming with life that very few people ever see! Take a peek at the animals that make their home in a tall, tall redwood tree.

Octopus Escapes Again—Swim along with Octopus as she searches for food and outwits dangerous enemies by using a dazzling display of defenses. Oh, yes, Octopus escapes again and again!

Pitter and Patter—Take a ride with two water droplets, Pitter and Patter, as they flow through the water cycle. Oh, the places you'll go and the creatures you'll see!

A Moon of My Own—An adventurous young girl journeys around the world, if only in her dreams. She discovers natural beauty and manmade wonders, accompanied by her companion—the moon.

There's a Bug on My Book—Children's imaginations will be engaged as they're introduced to all sorts of critters that hop, fly, wiggle, and slide across the pages of this book.

Wonderful Nature, Wonderful You—Nature can be a great teacher. With a light touch especially suited to children, this 20th Anniversary edition evokes feelings of calm acceptance, joy, and wonder.

Wild Ones: Observing City Critters—Follow the curious and adorable dog, Scooter, as he travels through an urban landscape seeing many wild animals, and not seeing many others.

Dawn Publications is dedicated to inspiring in children a deeper understanding and appreciation for all life on Earth. You can browse through our titles, download resources for teachers, and order at www.dawnpub.com or call 800-545-7475.